TENDER AGENCIES

TENDER AGENCIES

≈

DENNIS DENISOFF

ARSENAL PULP PRESS

VANCOUVER

ARSENAL PULP PRESS
100-1062 Homer Street
Vancouver, B.C.
Canada v6b 2w9

The publisher gratefully acknowledges the assistance of the Canada Council and the Cultural Services Branch, B.C. Ministry of Small Business, Recreation and Culture.

Cover design by Val Speidel
Cover photo by Conrad Poirier, courtesy of Archives nationales
    du Québec, Direction de Montréal, de Laval, de Lanaudière,
    des Laurentides et de la Montérégie
Typeset by Vancouver Desktop Publishing Centre
Printed and bound in Canada by Hignell Printing

CANADIAN CATALOGUING IN PUBLICATION DATA:

Denisoff, Dennis, 1961-
  Tender agencies

Poems.
ISBN 1-55152-012-5

  I. Title.
PS8557.E84T4 1994   C811'.54   C94-910727-1
PR9199.3.D46T4 1994

DEDICATIONS

"A Comprehensive Miner Murders the Power Source" is for Michael. "Who is Luis Possy?" is dedicated to Rob Dunham. I would like to thank Doris Zibauer for her invaluable research assistance for "The Skeletal Refrains: Bridge Game." Brief, distinguishable passages of various poems are taken from *Roget's Thesaurus*. Earlier versions of some of the poems in this collection have appeared in *East of Main*, *Mirage #4/Period[ical]*, *Sodomite Invasion Review*, and *West Coast Line*. I am grateful to the editors of these presses and journals for their support. I would also like to thank M. Morgan Holmes, Marina Bellanovskaya, George Bowering, Rob Dunham, Kevin Killian, Andy Levy, Lisa Robertson, Nancy Shaw, and Fred Wah, as well as the Kootenay School of Writing and its ever-extending community.

FLAUGHT:

i) A lock of hair. *English Ballad: "He's sent ye boys what ye lo'ed maist, A flaught o' his yellow hair."*

ii) A sudden blast; a flash (of lightning); a tongue of flame. Thus both insight and inconstancy. *Swinburne: "When your eyes Wax red and dark, with flaughts of fire between, I fear them."*

iii) A spreading out, as of wings for flight. A fluttering. *Disraeli: "His flaught into politics caught on the swelling wind of mass reform."*

iv) A flock of birds. Collective agency. Trusting reaction. *Hobbes: "Thus farre concerning the flaught; and how it cannot help but move in unison onely, the head having turned."*

v) With outspread wings; with great eagerness.

CONTENTS

WHO IS LUIS POSSY?

I mean besides dead. First cutting
(as if dissecting)
and then eating his words:
       We are being pushed to the
       brink. A little given, and
       a little something waiting.
       We are pushed, pushed ie:
come here you slimy chronofage:)

          Unbreakable Combs For Men

until the king of Egypt saw his own frail son
pass before him as a prisoner

to lay you on your back and deep pump you until
hot flick of a back lash

so then ie: EI EIO where:
       E equals moments of credence
       O equals moments of release
       Egypt as a square shadow of Eden
       (Frowned ewe's brow, having eaten

re: rereading the tableau vivant
come skulking
all his friends around him
frail, lamenting and releasing
(one spreads its wings
and they all do)
                        AIDS AS ACCESS TO INTIMACY
the light just so
chicken mesh of punctuation
(as opposed to the excitable
"This poem just dances rings around the grammar!"
(here a conscious of, there a conscious of

                                        a squint of green
                                        water-skiers in red
                                        swimsuits over the
                                        wakes

any poem has two enemies one
internal one external to
the text as over the weeks
death becomes a source
(up the staircase on his ass for example crying)

Luis or as my grandfather says.   Luis.
his embarrassingly depraved
lips flailing
furious
as intimate as a weakness
the masses not concerned but curious
break grief away from the voice
words as poison or perfume
depending on where you put them
he sure as fuck well

the elements and not the kettles (of course
how as you well know by now already of this design and how

"Hey waiter, I didn't order this.
Who ordered this and who brought it to *me*?"

My hand resting nearby
so that if he should decide or need to

the interior design supports
no design is owned
poetry is no longer something on the plate

       Possy's words become carnivores: Word off word.
       Image off image. Sunny side up. Grease as ease.
       Healthy as maggots. Success to the death (and
       always always St. Theresa's amber glow).
       Vulturous as anteaters. Somebody else's babies

lay him on his fetal side and straddle his hip firmly
as a saddler
first in Egypt
then in Nanaimo

pecs like car roofs

perhaps related to this remark is
the concept behind
the frail ancient painter's coffee round ass and soft curls

visibility to rough fuck
the masses as decisively derisive
up to one's elbows in it.   Luck.
delicacies
and soft curls of cheese
and capers and onions
and a whole done ham to gnaw on

> We want life since greed is chronological:
> edacity, esurience, gluttony, gormandizing, see
> insatiableness, see ravenousness, see voracity,
> see voluptuousness, see hunger

this pain here
that itch
this prolonged desire to
eat to
desire to
vomit
the masses not solicitous but obsequious

in desperation
on the death bed
the sky becomes more and more
Italy
this pale blue ancient failure
for you, I'll try:

                                        bulldog
                                        blue

the sun conched in the shell of ear
the crease on the lobe
the chrome on the tub

heaven shadows Egypt
some are jealous because fags are not
as ageless and instant as coffee
in a proper copper nipple

Aztecs burying their dogs
(but not the Spaniards
mother says don't let him bleed (on your white shirt or open wounds
"fags just eat and eat and eat and eat and eat and eat and eat and eat and

eat

dreams laid on palms like unwanted fish
possum fetus
chewing each other in contempt
too much cleanliness and dry will
runny breathing
(I remember this later and work it in)
a gentle tug through a sure fog
a gentle fag whose dense grey hair

but when a few days
afterward one of Al
exander's own men c
ame to die, hairles
s and helpless, par
ted, the cold windo
w sucking heat from
his grey cheek, his
eyes flaring like f
aghens barely aware
of the sepulcher, o

St. Paul S
t. Theresa
step out o   with a
f the bath   ll thi
water (luk   s know
e warm) an   ledge,
d shake on   who wo
it   uld wa
                       nt a y

a rabid spaniel's mouth clamps over the king, then he

                       amp, n   , the king, at last
                       o just   was wary and just o
                       a sand   r not simply so but
                       box fi   sad and filled with
                       lled w   unleashed remorse
                       ith an
entire Vienna boys choir
lashes out to here and o

COUNTRY IS PHOTOS

I.

a cut calendar sheet of Canada
a well-oiled pane
a field trip—let's sit in the back, eh?
just one subtle second here

> between a grain of snow and
> the sublime swirls of the w
> orld in arctic tidal pools.
> What a blurry shot. In and
> out. Up to old. Cold as c
> od. Slick as salmon. Beach
> ed. Lathered. Rather. Unt

2.

a letter
re: Sea of Love
one beat words
nothing propagating polysyllabicism
"Perhaps we had just made up and kissed."
no that's pumpkin not Pushkin
too glacial to recognize
the teacher says stand and spell.   Fridged.
had quavered and eaten a Mac.

3.

my potential photo
"This is saved—my jacket is on it."
I am a sprout a green tractor holding my own
the west behind me
am blinded but potent
tight at hips inundated at birth
with country
Anguish: a n g u i s h: very good
he knew only the back of his hand well
had managed to know it by the time he was older
and broader across the chest
you can sit down now
crows nest
"This is saved—see my jacket?"
Canadian as currently dated
sit down please
blinded my left arm slung plum over that mountain
a mossy tuft, a flake, a lock of hair or wool

potentially happy
the panorama trembles

4.

each ochre postcard
an obituary
cameras pan Canada as ferris wheels

> excuse me, nature as locusts not
> focus. A country with no seal
> nor impasse nor cul de sac. N
> o other otter nor wet warm hay
> fever. Plate tectonics not Pl
> otinus. No current. Stagnant
> pan of ram fat. The biggest c
> ountry you can't turn around i

manoeuvre my oppositional stance

                              dance that stompy way

wince

5.

the next postcard
folded
had languished and really
it all always occurs in a foreign country no bigger than
Great Slave Lake
beaver fever
Hey, your dam will bust! Your dam will overflow!
Who ordered them? I didn't order them and who drank them?
What are they?
drunk
C a s h e: no that is incorrect
You damn well sit

6.

the camera reel hits on
a blue baseball cap, a
squat silver dog licks a
condom, a lawn caller
against a red brick con
dominium and the whites

language: l   a   n   g   u   i   s   h: very good
my first window went with me cross country
once again the Canadian hero packs his mother
but not his traveller's cheques
mountain not Montaigne
oh please sit down
in Saskatchewan
I didn't know when to stop
                 whether to disclose my timidity

7.

another shot
it's not a perm but the humidity
I have to think back but I seem to
every lake or river with an Indian name
every aunt ending in Ann
longjohns not Longinus
oh boy, pot luck what!
to catch a fish as big as my son
had been agitated
empty black construction paper sheet of mosquitoes
shimmer of a double hook
two fish, hey! One for each hand
(boy you're a scrawny pictograph
data galore
had weakness for
quivered at a prong

8.

traditional Indian dress
I have never repeat never and never
want to hear that again
no dirt on the sealskin soles
Rhode Island Red headdress
Mabel Lacroix
Red currants galore

had shuddered, stamped and mailed it

Don't forget to press a leaf between these pages.

CONSUMER COMPLAINT

Thank you for contacting us with
your comments on our barbecued
chicken dogs. We have no idea.
                    —Ivory Snow (04/16/58)

Should that horrid beast succeed in getting through the open
window, my African violet will be the first to die.

weekend work
was always saved
for the other wealthy
pallidarians
            —Mr. Clean (02/28/74)

Thank you for contacting dogs. We appreciate both compliments and critiques as they help ensure high quality standards are maintained. Your comments have been recorded, the records were passed on to quality control, the control was

nothing pleasant
comes from the slick of milk
in a cup of cold coffee
                    —Kennel Ration (08/17/87)

I know that
you know that
close family relatives know that
but we're not concerned
with proximity
a unit until a union

Their report is given here.

She had the sudden compulsion to order anti-glare screens for everybody in the office.
control the pancreas

> That chicken was chopped less
> intentionally than you think: fowl
> cock hen pullet fryer broiler capon
> coward see cowardice see animal
> see food. Imperfection? Those
> white flecks are there for a purpose
> I'll have you know.

Whenever an x is used correctly in a sentence, another star in the sky tumbles to earth and becomes a street light, a counter-axis for the galaxies. Xxxxx. After a while the letter became nonconceptual and so terminated my employ.

dishwasher and oven safe
more lights in a big city than a small one
point being—no twinkle

My beard has finally covered the scars and I'm not looking back.
Xx.

why do you bring it up. maybe
you should deal directly with the
cashier. knives dishwasher safe.

It was so unlike her to run that that is what I remember most about
her—that and her breathing afterward.

I've mastered the fax and I'm not turning back. Xxxxx.

I can see one of his hairs on the windowsill so that makes me part
of his territory. Had I not seen it I would still be free.
from that.
        —handles of plastic (11/04/94)

29

Their report is given here.

life on the wiener line is a barrel of blood

> what are you doing. nobody else
> has complained. it tastes fine to us.
> we buy them all the time. by sunset
> he'll have peed on every house in
> Mount Pleasant. are you sure it was
> one of ours.

> the inevitable infiltration of the
> public voice by the private mind.
> fraught they taught us not with
> problems but with possibilities.

creators artworks and perceivers
> —my depression as Downy (3/23/98)

They take my vegetables away at the border because *verdurous* is
not in their dictionary.

Their report is given here.

did you buy it packaged or bulk.
have you kept a sample. what is the
code date. did you know the code
date is irrelevant. history hangs on
every word. it is there for the
manager—you should not touch
it. everything is illegal for your
sake, while in Mexico scrub
brushes grow on trees.

we only slaughter hogs, not
chickens. the meat is imported
from another planet. in our plant
we do not use metal matching your
description. the meat is important
for another reason. Scope. we bear
no responsibility. we bear no ill
feelings. We are willing.

we have made contact with them.
our meat is guaranteed.
        —S.O.S. Pads (07/13/08)
we are sorry it made you ill. their
quality control department has
been notified and is acting
appropriately. their report is here.
my dog has forgotten or is it back
to hard to get. thank you for

contacting our firm with your comments on our barbecued chicken dogs. this is rare. we don't know.

please accept our apologies for any inconvenience they might have caused. this is well done. the foreign object you found in the wiener has been sent to a private lab for unbiased analysis. they will take approximately. once again it has never happened before. history hangs on every word.

should the foreign object be associated with our production lines you will be hearing from our lawyers. payment of dental bills, days absent from work if proof of work is presented, medical bills for throat operations, any routine abdominal x-rays. there is just one small picture in our dictionary and anatomically we wonder. we will not pay for time spent at the doctor's or dentist's that could have been covered at night or on days off. Nor will we pay for suffering sufferance hurt cut discomfort painfulness malaise nightmare anguish agony excruciation torment torture rack distress affliction see adversity see disease see lamentation see dejection

boar scent. we'll have you know.
infiltrate the ecosystem. command
abort. send us the sample and we
will reply fully. or our agency will.
the thesaurus diagrammed the
meat dissected the blood collected
and analyzed. dog having eaten

A COMPREHENSIVE MINER
MURDERS THE POWER SOURCE

the train of miners
the steam of slit thigh in snow
stick match
bushels and bushels of black oily hair
"Look, a union. A union!"
then look at that

the emperor
left hand lightly over right
mistaking the breeze for a camouflage
mistaking my whispers for patchouli
political viburnum
the train of time
snowed in from Albany to Montréal
by dent of cheek
light years from the closest satellite photo
I came to the realization that would determine the course

snowed in
tiny miners
scrape frost off the night
veins pulse as I tap "m"
I tap "m" and the four and twenty elders
fall down pummelled

wait wait wait
Who wants to know and
why do you keep asking?
one starts a commotion and we all do it
that's how fault works
if we *all* do it, nobody gets blamed

my name all over it
my word given
(to make order, I say
Henry Mary Lady Jane Grey
enamoured and alluding
vial of veronal
spillikin flaming

A little letter with "Still alive in New York. Scrapers up to here. A cigarette burn in the red carpet of the eleventh floor of the Carlton belongs to me. The ochre girders within the bowels of Liberty. Or was it your absence. I'll tell you later. Later, I will be able to tell."

we are so exhaustive
you must not milk the words
we expect a lot in so few
days my slim veined foot
crushes opaque and white
linen juices
reduced to powder
words as flat as sheets of flesh
as transient as breath
and hush and still
a measure of barley for a penny
and three measures of barley for a penny
commerce whispers over me
this then is not salvation
is a late night transformation
from morality to ideology

pumice scrubbed
    ugly American cities roll off like kid dirt: Plattsburg Yonkers
    Saratoga Springs. Not all American cities are ugly. There are
    some further east I heard tell about.
give the vial a trial run
the train pierces the border with me
saying holy holy holy lord god almighty
which was and is and is to come watching
the steel toilet with its capped fluttering
"Elizabeth, James, then parliament"
purse strings taut

metal hands and shoulder blades
flat against the back wall
humming
waiting
humming
(as the emperor's turn to drink from the goblet approaches
lips pursed to a hummingbird
we have exhausted much in so few
all the Oranges for example
James then William and Mary then Anne was it Anne?
James's son

each eats steadily with marked action of jaws
a coiffed head cocked appears as alert as a bottle

and the number of them was ten thousand times ten thousand and thousands of thousands. All water-skiers. All aflock, a chain of arms bending at the pit. As the glass is raised and shimmering. Him humming. And the numbskulls waiting in and out of the shadows chomping at the bit. Letters of cheer dripping prematurely from their lips

left hand lightly over right alabaster fingers kneed
extended languishing
everything so glowing, white and sectioned
between 1879 and the winter
George George George George Victoria

very fortunate life" (as his sister-in-law later called it).)

tense cream calf over the bidet
crisp head lolling on enamel
along a small community of miners
this was happening and we were there
> Gravel for canaries. Marrow for dogs. Grovel for cherries.
> In as much as he could never or hoped for. Black oil on that
> thigh groove. Eels lounging, smoking, anxious for Elizabeth's
> death. And their power was to hurt men five months.

nature obscured by insufficient medical information
the artist at a distance painting by flashlight
the golden miners lolling muscles in Sudbury (Oh,

that is where they do that. Oh, that is *why* I did this) to the rhythm
of Edward George Edward George Edward Elizabeth. Hard drop
of honey dew melon. The emperor's dry lips part and exhale.
What was that he said? *Who* replaces him? The goblet shimmers
for moments

and the SKIES open for Michael
the voice of harpers harping with their harps
every last one of them water-skiers
white linen briefs with wide elastic waistbands
the train: "Klein Calvin Klein Calvin Klein Calvin Klein"
the station itself silent and gentle
frozen flanks
everyone asleep and breathing
while I sprinkle patchouli
in strategic corners

THE SKELETAL REFRAINS: BRIDGE GAME

mumbo
coming from these rooms:
parlour, parliament, and nation
wiping egg off on the apron
poachers have reduced Africa but ah
the skeleton remains tender
(icing on the cupcake
straw on the bad back
eye on the spoon
jawbone nearby
bloody
sutured
fessed up
the animals created
named
left waiting to wander
recitative (mezzo-soprano)
then shall the eyes of the blind
be opened, and the ears

jumbo and trainer Winston
Winston and his little assistant Scotty
their fistal love
his father's house
who invited him? the dip
the chips, everything seems to be out
the soft hands of the Kraft lady
deal the cards, crystal clean, serve
the Winter Marshmallow Delite

> The elephants knew of the emperor's soft spot, his
> sensitive flutter of skin, so they were not surprised when
> he returned, tired and puffing, his right hand briskly
> unhooking the grey silk of his gown from the thistles it
> caught along the dusty roadside, then quickly shifting
> lightly over left, covering the wounds.

October 1989 officially endangered
delighted slips from the oven
Zimbabwe, Botswana, and Burundi fold
Switzerland rejoices and dips a salt and vinegar
pass him the sponge
he's cross

limbo
welcome to New York
raw poached ivory easy over
elephants, raise your trumpets
the emperor has a soft spot in which to hook your tusks
the thralls' flaught pending, pending, pending
the third story window last one on the left
marked MENS
streets like canyons off the dock
thousands throng
the diminutive clown elephant
what you know and what you hope
humming
waiting
humming (as the trumpeter turns to drink from the fountain
an unscheduled Grand Trunk train sears from the fog

dumbo
every creature that moveth
Jebel Ali Freeport is a household word
so is "Move it. Come on, move it."

       at night men creapeth from small boats in hopes of easy
       penetration. I am out back leaking into the local
       economy. the citizens dance. the moon drips.

every nation has an outback
it is sew and it is knot
stitch and suture
legal tender
Jumbo's fatal collision with a Grand Trunk train
fetal but steaming

       "Oh Winston, oh Winston. The
       body is hollow. The walls are
       seven thick. My train of thought
       is solid steel."

air (bass) the trumpet shall sound
kings, queens, what's trump
this is a picture of the camera I used
but the photos were confiscated

sombre
the quilled texture is achieved by trowelling
the legs and the base are poured
sections are later joined at the site
two large tractor-trailer trucks
two large tractor-trailer trucks
stuck out back leaking

is because responsible
I reach tenderly with my trunk

> "Oh Scott, oh Scott. Devoted
> friend between faithful thralls. My
> mounted hide travels in circles.
> My skin is destroyed when the
> circus burns."

the skeleton remains on display
Scotty dreaming of Winston's fist
tusks like curled and wilting lilies
continue to slip the circuit

(but now stiff as) mortish

I once again bring thrills and
pleasure to visitors of every age. I
cannot remember the cool
savannah, smell of cahana, shells of
New York, scent of new elephants
corralled and rounded up

waltz and waltz of thrills and dips
buffalo boys shoot out
their lips shake
their heads saying,

brave like bull
dumb like streetcar

strumpet
Mr. X still sells ivory to A.B.
who stands on the warehouse roof
recalls the stars and street lights
she trumpets when she's happy she trumpets when she's sad
    you talk to her
where's a rhino?

> upon visiting the factory they
> discover that the ivory is not
> stacked to the ceiling and though
> worms destroy this body yet in my
> flesh shall I see
>   —God (Job 19: 25-26)

oh pray, oh mulch, oh poach mon flesh
what the worms say

while distantly
Scott reaches up for his drunk
and a new crowd alights

PROXY

I wouldn't know a good shoe shine if it hit me in the face
not wishing to enter the convent she sits down on the stone steps
scrapes at the scabs between her toes
as she attracts the shadows of buildings

twice the traffic slaps her
here, here
and near here
near the agency

> One can be preponderantly motivated to *A*—and
> even believe that this motivation will effectively
> motivate an *A*-ing—without simultaneously
> being decided upon *A*-ing. I am in this
> motivation/belief condition with respect to
> aiding the child; but I am not decided upon
> aiding her.

the pain from a distance is searing
that I know nobody
that makes me an accomplice

it is all in the proximity of my life
and the pain in my stomach
why even frown

> (once again I spend the better part of the morning
> getting to work. The best part getting off the bus.

hold the map steady and point the arrow north
once she spins and once she falls

        (on seeing blood I repeat in my head there is a
        serious line between the world as image and the
        world imagined

I only say it twice before I calm down in public

        (in the Soviet Union (and elsewhere I now know)
        buses are made to bend around corners at ran-
        dom, thereby making maps utterly useless

in the proximity of   30 dollars
broken watch battery   hospitality quotient

        Agents deliberate carefully about means of
        assistance and intentionally take measures to
        counter the pull of unruly desires, even when they
        think that their chances of success are low-
        moderate. In such cases—if the propulsion of the
        collective flaught is either unlearned or
        dissipated—the agents do *not* intend to *A*.
        Dissipation of the collective flaught, as we have
        seen, is itself the result of an intentional measure
        functioning within a subterfuge of collectivity.

remove even the face
the agency
the scalpel
and the cattle flock to see the sleeping child
what were the criteria *before* you were elected

the best art is made to fit
the obvious reason is speed and convenience
that means it rots
shedding
the law says bears eat critters and we shoot bears
bears eat and eat and eat and eat and eat and eat and eat and eat and eat
and nobody in *my* town is in any big hurry to get to the moon
something is given and something is conceived
we act on an assumed flaught
but we still only act

> in my own defense, even if intending to A does not depend
> upon one's having decided to A, we are strongly disinclined
> to believe that someone *x*, who is resolved upon resisting
> his desire to A, *intends* to A. Agents who are more strongly
> motivated to *A* than not to *A* sometimes actively resist
> their motivation to *A*. *X*, or someone like *x* can be, and
> generally is, demotivated by the collective itself. However,
> the collective flaught, the fluttering valve of automatonism,
> perpetrates individual agency.

if I've got to look it up
somebody else had better use it

here boy is presumptuous
I know

a dead husband more than anything else
is a widow. most of us tend to forget that

hopping scared

the girl is dying I can tell
cross your living room and hope
        the church I like is the Ukrainian Catholic one
        on Mount Pleasant with a cupola that can be
        either a nipple or a penis, a rabbit or a duck
miraculously the line-up at the bank machine dwindles
the dying girl's mother has chosen to go *there* to pray
        mother taught us at an early age the difference
        between staring and not blinking. The little
        girl blinked. We all did
accounts of intentional behaviour appeal to agents' beliefs,
desires, wishes, decisions, plans, sometimes to deliberation.
        Her study, with her cane and box cap, the blotter
        she used and the quill found in her breast pocket
        at death. Even the aquarium shattered and shard
is not my fault
        not surprisingly there are no words on page 9
        subtle enough to differentiate pain sufferance
        hurt cut discomfort painfulness malaise nightmare
anguish agony excruciation torment torture rack
        distress affliction see adversity see lamentation
        see dejection see disease see hell

this Malay night
I can't describe
but try

dark
blueish

[I know,
the dog's tongue freezes by a flashlight on the back porch
the blood expands to fill the body]

HE SANG HIM

What are you looking for?
What have you lost dear?

remember my forgotten man he sang

    remember
        my forgotten man

the kid the kid the kid the kid
.green green green green green.
the kid the kid the kid the kid
the kid the kid the kid the kid
.green green green green green.
the kid the kid the kid the kid

starring three garish young lawyers
all green in the streetlight
gargled into their best suits
(THEY suited *them* and *they* suited THEM)
singer gangs

"Well then we all just cast our underwear
        back at the audience
                oh how we laughed
                        you see we were drinking pernod that year
                    the entire cast
                      well at least I was
                        oh how we laughed then, you see
                    they knew us
                    we were known
                      each of our stomachs
                    flat enough
                 ʳ to eat
                  off of o

I remember that Theresa, before becoming a saint, always tilted her head lightly to the left when receiving the host so that one side of it touched her pale pink meat first, and began to melt first, and slid down her throat first, throwing the men in the deep red capes off balance. Once she became a saint, of course, they tore her head off.

the kid the kid the kid the kid
.green green green green green.
the kid the kid the kid the kid

he was
Percy was explaining
sleeping with his brother
the subpoena, the subpoena!
we all crawled from the wreckage
flocked to the trailer
transparent evasions
scattered across the linoleum
(peonies
pin-feathers
cut by a grid, or grill
none of us could understand
how we hadn't noticed before
Mr. Gilbert crowed and crowed
Mr. Gilbert is damned thought I
(little bubbles leading to my big bubble

"Once he used to love me. I was happy then."

forgetting him sang he
means you're forgetting me

while Percy swore off shaving
little dogs lapped up the blood
the words falling from her breath "hE
was *never* a star

They came off the beach and Billy was steaming you know the way
he can just sort of haughty and his legs especially long and Johnny
with that downier hair on the inside of his thighs said pointing well
I'm never going for a walk with *his* abdomen again. How we
laughed that year. When Billy became really ill, it was by the
abdominals that we measured his deterioration. When he finally
died, of course, his bowels went totally slack.

But if you'll excuse me
how do we know that wasn't
a question of course   the kid the kid the kid the kid
                                  .green green green green green.
he loved his brother   the kid the kid the kid the kid
he's knitting a green scarf for his grave
striped knit one pearl one you know
it's cold in them there hills   the kid the kid the kid the kid
a scarf for his slim white   .green green green green green.
                                    the kid the kid the kid the kid
a scarf as long as the beach   .green green green green green.
                                    the kid the kid the kid the kid

I felt it appropriate and told him so
I always spoke my mind
that year when I was still worthy
where is everyone

Lyricism and narcissism?
No, I didn't know
I should write that down

but then they suddenly told us all to go back
back then they had always taught us to go for poignancy

— the way a person with Alzheimer's can say "My mind is going
    like it's separate from the body
    like it's going
    over there
    somewhere entirely
    off the gazebo

— like the middle-aged man in the L.A. earthquake who kept
   combing his hair over his bald spot and who said, "I'm all
   shook up" and laughed and then began to cry

— like Tallulah Bankhead lays herself across his thighs in *Lifeboat*,
   drills her finger through the words

— the ease with which I knit him a scarf on the computer because
   that's the only way I know how

— the way a person whose mind is gone says "My mind is going."

— the ease with which manatees continue being chopped by the
   propellers of motorboats in Florida swamps

— the poignancy with which their blood flows and disappears

— like the pleading lunatic says,
    when he's told that he'll have to be put away,
    "But yet you assume that I understand *that!*"

MID POST

the peas of Kiev are unshelled but packaged
positioned
gently lined
amongst the grid of white linoleum

by now
the window   by how
sills   the wind
spin so   nonnuclear
mixedly   thins so
everybody retires to the safety of the bed   quickly
pow   everybody has separate access to the bed
                                                                 post

creamy yet dry to the touch
the cheek of that frozen calf
we are told not to eat

with more news on the radio than in the world
I find the stupid church across the street
                    quaint warm
                    squarish banal

ax-
like
root
rising
totem pole-like a
mammoth Ukrainian salt
bowl hand carved, hand painted,
garish red and light crossing the
horizon and not really rising at all
it calms me just to know it calms
all those folks down
cupola brimming
with calm
    a calm autumn evening
    language leaping calmly
      in sense as well as time
        size as well as degree

9.5   9.8   9.7   9.7   9.8   9.8   9.9   9.85   9

locals busily spraying not voting
lips brimming with cum

my computer not the colour of
any nun in particular

Vancouver proper considerably
less peripheral
better supplied

I will not tolerate children who say
I hate you I hate you I hate you I hate you I hate you

as bed time is a moment
that is to say
make a sturdy life

I don't like trauma. What makes you think I like trauma?

Each one sees one's own position in
relation to the victims as most
suspect. A few hope so and that's
valid if you knew them, each sensing
the flutter of skin inspiring the
collective flaught

any group overconsumes
madam

he doesn't notice Marge
take more time than necessary
(though lacking lobes
he still inspired jewellery)
galena earrings
from the real to the realized
the real not anywhere
until warranted

some statements made
while waiting for word:

Everything took Tolstoy so long.

If Tolstoy had been born in Shelley's age he would have
been dead by now.

My childhood recollections have never ended.

Any memory retrieved, is first something forgotten.

By this definition in:
    "You are late again. You did not get here *in* time."

You do not *want* to learn. You are dreaming.

68 Detail of 62.

Not everyone in Québec is named Pierre.
Some are named Alain.

everything nowadays
rendered with a realism
beyond virtuosity

rear-ender brought screams
as a murder brings to mind
darkling meltdown
faith in the real

there is plenty of time for that
but not enough time for this

I pop in on Oly to look at the blender
face the colour of anything pureed
all the peas shelled
arranged
a line from the bed to the toilet
edge of a table cloth handkerchief
limpidity of snot putting me on edge

every star not used in the language
We ensure that each binary star is individually shelled.

in olden days upon a time like when
assuming they even
let
you
in

Not everyone in Québec is named Pierre.
I know someone named Alain.

locals busily voting not cheating

Sophie carries on solitary talks with herself that she swears could not without damage to the integrity of the discourse be immediately translated into dialogue.

holidaying in Montréal
mother notes "the subtlety of the French"

> After years of research they finally began storing all the televisions with better commercials in a safe in the basement of the metropolitan library.

until a safer date such as when at which time
I'm not in on it
not in time
in time
ime
ime int
ime int not
in ont not me

The high point of his career came
with the recognition that a fart
sounded the same before and after the
creation of language.

When the melt down does I am
reciting English text and appreciate
their gifts of water and ripe oranges.

locals busily musing not cheating

a cloud track of chickadees
dead tubers
stiffed in flaught
splotched in dung
few things are like and I make no exceptions
pointing at the reindeer with a mechanical eye
more correctly translated?
not until I am told
locals busily eating not cheating

though by the window
attention is not on the sill
Oly pukes on it right away

Let me make it clear right from the start
nothing surprises me any more
except a fresh firm plum the size of my fist

HALLELUJAH PANCAKE SYRUP

I'm sorry
I'm sorry
phase of superiority
pastoral elegy:
springs of agency
pigs sneeze and dehydrate

(jug)
the 20th century as a dry run
Upon birth you realize you have been dead until then
at which point after which

What do you paint—portraits or landscapes?
Putts.
Hallelujah.

rakish
that man is rakish
this man is svelt
another man is that man is he is that guy sure is boy is he ever

pound cakes   *pork drippings*   *god box versus*
bed box   *vittles*   *pea syrup*

listen
do you hear that?

dot MAtrix dot MAtrix

it is the amber-tipped boxfinch
begging for water
its clear crisp voice can be heard in most of the marshes in
Siberia and even in areas west of the Urals
note perfect phenomena
(in the background—
the tongueless nightingale)

a pillow over a maple pew
a sinew of his stuck between my teeth
computers men and carnivores
vs. god box full of red sea oils
asterisks replace pork rinds
corn cakes

they	found	him		at		the	carnival
absinthe	sodden	and		dead		til	26
I		like	this	arm		which	is

mine

this just came over the wire
the more I try wash them off the more I recall
lower case letter ts across the god box
datta. data
kneeling over the keyboard
succumbing to the amber glow of the monitor

this water has a funny taste
jug jug jug
pitcher
crossing the keyboard with scented feet

In a line, the novel is guilty. The novel makes excuses
to dead religion. The removal of guilt via innocence,
secondariness, constant refutation, fantasy, farce, buf-
foonery, burlesque, travesty, mockery, fiasco, see wit,
see drama.

phase to equality
gender and the size of the nose
gender and the whiteness of cuticles
gender and pitch
sperm and putt
pitcher in hand

would you rather I instead of as an alternative to

        we arrived late at the Red Sea

Delilah and her disposable camera
the aggression inherent to "Yes, but

poetry no longer something to wear
fell apple yellow to the grass dew taxed
now do you eat this apple or the connotations
something washes over me and I can't wash it off

poetry is no longer something to consume
hey I woke up and didn't remember a thing okay?
words as boxes bound in yellowed scotch tape
kIno komEdia
do you hear that

                                       swallow
its rich, clear notes can be heard here in the Taiga, in the
marshes and even in large cities with computers

            Spring marsha-hosanna, it is Spring

the fresh rust leaves on the maple trees
the divine scent of moist manure still in the air
warmed fresh fiddleheads hurl upward and curl back

onomatopEEia onomatopEEia

do you hear that?
it is the northern cuckoo
its clear crisp computer etc.
in the distance—lake frogs and a cock

at last something has come over me
shut that god damned box
no I'll do it
what's that smell
pew

                                        amber asterisk amber asterisk

hear that? (Philomela)
        not drinking
        not telling
        a nose   *a cuticle*   *a note*

FISSURE HIM HIM (SMACK DAB)

he stands in this
whirlwind,   my
entire head a bloody
pool amongst the
tears the laundry
mat the neurons
and he says and
then I repeat after
him:

CNS 14x PNS

but the mouth is not
in synch with the
words, the words
dribble aside, only
some juices pass
through and I do
not know whether
they are desired

they move my vision
up over there

AIDS has opened the door to a new
generation of emotions

FLAUNT YOUR GIRTH

he crawls over me like a hundred cats
pearl
I cannot nor have I ever
far from flowing over you
they crush for trusting the author
thrilled to talk
cat's sucking breath
I took to her
I look forward to the year 2000
(how else I ask you
who to follow

slim pale and waxing
Galaxy 500
strategically framed by thin, by tone, by time

nosing into my asterisk
thrilled to the flaunt
I see now this is not where I had started out with
                    rated   highest   in
                    synapse   rich   areas,
                    next in cell body rich
                    areas, lowest in axon
                    rich areas
I just love the words we exchanged yesterday:
position / emission / holography
stationary vehicle
nothing limp
enthralled he tells me
cherry lip balm
maybe something streamlined and hemmed
not the pillar of the community
but as thrilled as a flying buttress
Eros has arose. Hazard those in neurosis' sorrows
right smack dab between
explaining myself
a sudden blast of wind
licorice. puppies, chicks, lice and slugs.

neither was the young man more impressed by the baroque exterior
than the painting itself
(shuffle, shuffle, shuffle)
I did try to learn from the movies
honest
the reality of the frame
I am told later
is the artist's best clue
does infinitive mean seamless or productive?
as productive it is the last thing that should be split
I look forward to the furthest point
ironing me out

let's think of an example of this and hide it
    —   who to vote for
    —   whether to buy a pumpkin now
          or wait until tomorrow
          when the price goes down
    —   fuschia 3x>white

indirectly you must try understand in a way it cannot be denied
that

I could point it
out a million
times and I still
wouldn't want
you to see it.
The line the
tailor the drop
of hip. The
web between the
thumb and
forefinger.
The hair of
a porcupine. I,
I mean we, are
taking the
language in
oppositionally.
Infiltration
a n d
contamination.

We may choose
to capitalize
the O in power,
or we may not.
This is our
decision. The
drop of hip,
conversely, is
our desire.
O u r
uncontrollable
spreadsheet.

while the
possessive
always remains
misplaced,
always remains
owned by some
one else.

some say a story some say a continuous episode
he converged on the asterisk
he punctuated it and I never thought of it
(a special place to carry change?)
I have no interest in pressing that

hope, hatred and despair
converge in my bathroom
and begin plotting

pucker
god such localisation of foci
the vulgar light blue ring
Laika falls from my fingertips
or does killer?
Rilke

Just "he said" and already the community tears
the struggle of the evening train
the fastest objection the world
this roll of film
will be photos of me
when I was younger
will be   when   I was
2000 years later the plane takes off

if you could touch something
you are not in the air
by my book
what could an urban dog have to bark at
a nun   the brain   the fingertips

I am taking it
all with me. I
paid for it
with my own
money. Lowest
in axon rich
areas. Low at
b i r t h .
Increases with
maturation. I
paid for it
fair   and
square. I paid
for it cash
down. I paid
for it dot
matrix.

2000 years later planes alight
See, I can paint it but I cannot touch it
   — nightly square dancers kick up their heels
   — burn their ginch
   — the painting suspended by a bootstrap
   — the gritty wire inside the bulb
   — the straight line between the top of a pine
   — the tongue tip of lightning as it recoils from my butt
   — a brief eel on the black harbour
really all of it is trying
all tactical flaught
I don't care
it was made for expulsion
that's all we're good at

and wonder meant something to them
oh golly and men die before women
and the youth of today are younger than I
younger than I was
at their age

now that I've given up
but that I'm an utter failure
he said tearing like an old tent
"I can walk" Mary replied
dragging herself from the burning century
real estate agency
neither totally dejected
"No not bronzer not bronzer no!"
alighting not with the flair
of any well-fed Danish general
I still care
was earnestly calling for a reason?

everybody still tenderly awaits
(their passive maws agape)
the turquoise cowlick of divers

DENNIS DENISOFF lives in Montréal, where he is completing his Ph.D. in English at McGill University. He is the author of the novel *Dog Years* and the editor of *Queeries: An Anthology of Gay Male Prose*, both published by Arsenal Pulp Press.